LATIMER STUDIES 77

THE ETHICS

OF USURY

BY BEN COOPER

The Latimer Trust

Published by the Latimer Trust January 2012

The Latimer Trust (formerly Latimer House, Oxford) is a conservative Evangelical research organisation within the Church of England, whose main aim is to promote the history and theology of Anglicanism as understood by those in the Reformed tradition. Interested readers are welcome to consult its website for further details of its many activities.

The Latimer Trust
London N14 4PS UK
Registered Charity: 1084337
Company Number: 4104465
Web: www.latimertrust.org
E-mail: administrator@latimertrust.org

CONTENTS

I.   Introduction

In the wake of the 'sub-prime' crisis which hit the financial world in 2008, this is hardly a favourable time to be defending the practice of lending and borrowing money at interest. The bizarre background to the crisis has now been told many times, but the basic story is this.[1] With rising house prices at the end of the 1990s and credit becoming dramatically less expensive around the turn of the century, mortgage lenders in the United States began to market increasing numbers of so-called 'sub-prime' loans. Sub-prime lending is lending directed at people with very low credit ratings. Such loans therefore have a higher risk of default, but are made at higher rates of interest. By 2007, these loans accounted for 13-14% of the market. It should have been obvious at this time that the expansion of the sub-prime sector had become dangerously reckless.[2] Partly, the recklessness was because those offering the loans had little incentive to make sure they were made honestly. The loans were "securitized"; that is, they were pooled, repacked and then sold on to other investors in a secondary market. The pooling and repackaging was intended to remove the risk from the loan, apparently turning a high-risk, high-return loan into a low-risk, high-return loan. This of course made them very attractive to investors. However, as those receiving the original loans began to default on their mortgage payments, it quickly became apparent that the devices used to remove the risk from them had been poorly designed and, indeed, never properly tested. The true value of the repackaged loans turned out to be massively less than investors had thought when they bought them. Many investors, including some prominent banks, found themselves under severe

---

[1]   The clearest and most readable account I have come across is John Lanchester, *Whoops! Why Everyone Owes Everyone and no One Can Pay* (London: Penguin, 2010).

[2]   For example, some 60% of sub-prime applicants in 2006 were exaggerating their income by more than 50%. Lanchester, *Whoops!* p 111.

financial pressure. This then led to a wider crisis in the global credit market, the effects of which are still being felt deeply in many Western economies.

Of course, sub-prime secured lending does not just hurt lenders. It also hurts borrowers. David Clough *et al* describe some of the ways in which sub-prime lending has hurt borrowers in both the UK and the US.[3] Some of this lending is now officially classified in the US as "predatory lending," and has resulted in large numbers of vulnerable people facing extraordinary costs.[4]

The image of lending and borrowing money at interest has also been marred by what seem to be hugely excessive levels of consumer borrowing in many Western economies. The charity Credit Action estimate that personal debt in the UK (excluding mortgages) averaged around £8,000 per household in August 2011. Averaged across households that actually have some sort of unsecured loan, the figure rises to £15,000.[5]

Against this background, it would be impossible to argue that the practice of lending and borrowing money at interest is *always* morally acceptable. Frequently, such practice is morally indefensible. Lending at interest *can* cause harm. As we shall consider further below, there are clear biblical injunctions against the kind of lending that exploits borrowers, as in what has become known as "predatory lending." Moreover, if borrowing is driven by lazy management, impatience or greed then of course we cannot countenance it. Greed, we should remember, is placed alongside the very worst kinds of sexual immorality by the apostle Paul (1 Corinthians 5:11, 6:9-10). "For the love of money is a root of all kinds of evils," he says

---

[3] David Clough, Richard Higginson, and Michael Parsons, "Usury, Investment and the Sub-Prime Sector," *Association of Christian Economists Discussion Papers* DP001 (2009): pp 5–7.

[4] See below (Section 5.1.1) for the definition of "predatory lending" used by the US General Accounting Office.

[5] URL: <http://www.creditaction.org.uk/helpful-resources/debt-statistics.html>. Accessed 01/08/2011.

elsewhere. "It is through this craving that some have wandered away from the faith and pierced themselves with many pangs" (1 Timothy 6:10). Is the biblical answer then simply to say "No" to the practice of lending and borrowing money at interest? That is, from a personal point of view, should we never indulge in the practice? As Lord Polonius puts it in *Hamlet:*

> Neither a borrower nor a lender be;
> For loan oft loses both itself and friend,
> And borrowing dulls the edge of husbandry.[6]

And then, having eschewed such practice in our personal (and church) lives, should we then campaign vehemently against such trade in the public sphere?

It would be fair to say that for the major part of church history the mainstream answers to these questions from Christian teachers have been strongly against the practice of borrowing and lending at interest. The church fathers vehemently condemned what has traditionally been called "usury" (that is, any interest made on a loan), attacking especially loan-making which sought to profit from the economic vulnerability or unexpected poverty of others (cf. the biblical material in Section 5.1 below).[7] Medieval scholastic theologians went even further, arguing that interest payments were intrinsically unjust. Aquinas maintained, for example, that "Making a charge for lending money is unjust in itself, for one party sells the other something non-existent, and this sets up an inequality which is

---

[6] *Hamlet,* Act I, Scene III. But note that Polonius is presented by Shakespeare as a bore and a busybody, so it is not obvious that he would have been in personal agreement with the advice!

[7] For example: Tertullian , *Against Marcion,* IV, 17; Cyprian, *Testimonies* III, 48; Basil, *Second Homily on Psalm 15;* Gregory of Nyssa, *Fourth Homily on Ecclesiastes;* Ambrose, *On the Duty of Clergy* III, 3.3; Chrysostrom, *Homilies on Genesis,* XLI; *Homilies on 1 Corinthians,* XIII; *Homilies on 1 Thessalonians,* X; *Homilies on Matthew,* V, LVI. All these texts can be found at URL: <http://www.ccel.org>.

contrary to justice."[8] Pope Benedict XIV argued that economic justice required the same quantity to be returned as was loaned.[9] The attack on usury was continued among the Reformers by Luther, most graphically in a sermon of 1519, which was published in a revised form in 1520 and then again, with additional material, in 1524, as *On Trade and Usury*.[10] In England, Hugh Latimer likewise spoke out strongly, saying, "For usury is wicked before God, be it small or great; like as theft is wicked."[11]

However, since the Reformation, something has clearly changed. Christians today happily take out mortgages and keep their money in banks which then lend at interest to others. They may even personally profit from the lending of money at interest. There are very few pastors who would rebuke them for such activity (and no doubt a majority who simply join in) and very few pulpits resounding with the anti-usury message of a Luther or a Latimer.

There are several ways in which one could respond to this change of attitude. One would be to see it as a humane ethical evolution. Usury was once seen as simply wrong, but as capitalism has brought growth and relief from poverty for many, Christians have had to revise their opinion. For many, it seems that usury is now only

---

[8]   *Summa Theologica*, 2.ii, Question 78, Article 1. Like Aristotle before him, Aquinas struggled with the idea that money could be just as real as the things it buys, even if that is by social convention. The *Summa Theologica* can be found online at URL: <http://www.newadvent.org/summa/>.

[9]   Benedict XIV, *On Usury and Other Dishonest Profit*, which can be found at URL: <http://www.papal encyclicals.net/Ben14/b14vixpe.htm>. Accessed 04/08/2011. This is not a very good argument, because a sum of money available to me now is more valuable than the same sum at some time in the future. I therefore incur a cost in lending it out. If economic justice requires at least that parties cover their costs, then an interest payment of some sort should be made. (This principle is known as "time preference" in modern discussion, and to adjust sums according to time preference is known as "discounting.")

[10]   Martin Luther, "Trade and Usury 1524," *Luther's Works*, (Michigan: Cordordia, 2011), vol 45 pp 240-310.

[11]   Hugh Latimer, *The Fifth Sermon on the Lord's Prayer*. URL: <http://www.ccel.org/ccel/latimer/sermons. ix.v.html>. Accessed 04/08/2011.

sometimes wrong, regardless of what the Scriptures say. The same principle can then be applied to other ethical issues. Listen, for example, to David Greenberg:

> If, in the course of the centuries, Christians were to modify or abandon some early doctrines (such as the prohibition of usury and, for Protestants, priestly celibacy), why not all? In some parts of the world, religious prohibitions against homosexuality are virtually ignored. Why has this not been so in the West?[12]

The history of the Christian attitude to usury then becomes a step in an argument for ethical revision in other areas.

An alternative response to the apparent change in attitude would be to throw up our arms in despair at the contemporary moral laxity of Christians on this issue, and call for a return to the prohibition. In the UK, the Jubilee Centre has been persistent in such a campaign.[13] The conservative evangelical magazine *The Briefing* recently included an article suggesting a return to interest-free living.[14]

However, there is a different approach, which is to argue that current Christian practice in Western economies is *not necessarily* at odds with biblical teaching. On this view, the hostility of Christian teaching on usury up to and including the Reformation was right in condemning bad practice, but wrong to suggest a *blanket* prohibition against lending at interest. Some kinds of lending at interest have *always* been permissible. This line of thought begins most prominently with John Calvin, who argued explicitly that there is no

---

[12]   David F. Greenberg, *The Construction of Homosexuality* (Chicago: University of Chicago Press, 1990), p 13.

[13]   Beginning with Paul Mills, *Interest in Interest: The Old Testament Ban on Interest and Its Implications for Today* (Cambridge: Jubilee Centre Publications, 1993). Many other resources are available online at URL: <http://www.jubilee-centre.org/resources>.

[14]   Andrew Schmidt, "Matters of Interest," *The Briefing (UK Edition)* vol 389 (February 2011) pp 10-13.

biblical teaching that "totally bans all usury."[15] Moreover, while clearly aware of the abuses of usury, he understood better than the scholastics that charging interest need not be economically unjust:

> If the debtor have protracted the time by false pretenses to the loss and inconvenience of his creditor, will it be consistent that he should reap advantage from his bad faith and broken promises? Certainly, no one, I think, will deny that usury ought to be paid to the creditor in addition to the principal, to compensate his loss. If any rich and monied man, wishing to buy a piece of land, should borrow some part of the sum required of another, may not he who lends the money receive some part of the revenues of the farm until the principal be repaid? Many such cases daily occur in which, as far as equity is concerned, usury is no worse than purchase.[16]

The final thought here, that in many cases "usury is no worse than purchase," will feature strongly in the analysis below. Trade in loans is much like other kinds of buying and selling. Just as all kinds of trade may be corrupted by dishonesty, greed or exploitative behaviour, so may the trade in loans. But just as trade in general is not necessarily a bad thing, and may in many cases work for mutual benefit, so it is in the trade for loans.

Calvin's more measured approach was continued by Matthew Henry: "Where the borrower gets, or hopes to get, it is just that the lender should share in the gain."[17] As noted above, generally speaking, mainstream Protestantism since the Reformation has at least implicitly subscribed to it. It has been defended in at least two recent

---

[15] J. Calvin, "Letter to Claude Sachin," in *Calvin's Ecclesiastical Advice* (eds. M. Beaty and B.W. Farley; 1545; repr., Edinburgh: T&T Clark, 1991), p 140.

[16] J. Calvin, *Commentaries on the Four Last Books of Moses Arranged in the Form of a Harmony, Volume III* (trans. C. W. Bingham; Edinburgh: Calvin Translation Society, 1852–55), p 131.

[17] Matthew Henry, *Commentary* on Deuteronomy 24. URL: <http://www.ccel.org/ccel/henry/mhc1.Deu.xxiv. html>. Accessed 04/08/2011.

studies.[18] And, much as it pains me to side with Calvin against Latimer in a *Latimer Study* on this issue, the current study represents an expanded restatement of this view.

2. The current study

The current study is an exercise in biblical ethics, revisiting the biblical data on lending and borrowing at interest according to certain principles. The scope of the study is deliberately limited. I shall not be attempting a detailed ethical assessment of every possible kind of debt contract or the arrangements surrounding them. For example, the issues surrounding debt *cancellation* (both biblical, as in Deuteronomy 15:1-11, and in contemporary application), interesting and important though they are, are beyond the scope of this study, and we can address the main questions in view without extensive reference to them.[19] These questions are as follows:

(1) What can we say about the principles behind the biblical prohibitions of lending at interest?

(2) Does the contemporary application of those prohibitions imply that it is *never* right to lend at interest?

(3) If not, then in what circumstances might lending at interest be permissible – or even beneficial?

The guidelines and principles under which these questions will be answered are explained in more detail in Section 4 below. In brief, they are: first, that the legislation on charging interest in the Mosaic Law *does* have an on-going moral significance for Christians; but, second, that biblical ethics needs to be done "perspectivally," taking account of personal and situational changes between the point of

---

[18] By, for example, Clough, Higginson, and Parsons, "Usury" and Thomas Renz, "Theses on Usury Then and Now" (2008), https://sites.google.com/site/thomasrenz02/usury.

[19] Having said that, I shall be commenting briefly on the foreigner-brother distinction in Deuteronomy 15:3 below.

legislation and the point of application. In the conclusions, I shall claim that the biblical answer to the question of usury expresses two further principles. These are not principles of interpretation, but ethical principles embedded in the answer that can be argued to apply more widely. The first of these is that the obligations between one individual and another depend to some extent upon the "moral proximity" between them. The second is that ethical study in any situation not *directly* addressed in the Scriptures should be done under the "doctrine of carefulness," exercising caution whenever we have any doubts about how to apply it.

Putting these together, the restatement of Calvin's position I shall be defending in what follows is this:

1. *Exploitative* lending, which targets and profits from individual vulnerability or weakness, is clearly prohibited for all time and all situations by God through the Scriptures. Moreover, it is easy for us to see how such lending is harmful and damaging to peoples' lives. (I shall define what is meant by "exploitative" more carefully below, Section 5.1.1)

2. However, there is no *blanket* ban on lending and borrowing at interest in the Bible and there do exist situations today where the practice is not exploitative, but rather mutually beneficial for the parties concerned, with potential for benefits more widely. For Christians, lending at interest *can* be a way of extending how much they are able to benefit others beyond what they are able to give or lend freely.

3. To reduce the possibility of relationally destructive exploitative lending, the Scriptures imply *carefulness*. That is, the practice of lending and borrowing at interest should be restricted to relatively distant, anonymous, "non-neighbour" transactions, where the parties involved have low "moral proximity," and where both parties can be confident the trade will be beneficial and prudent for the other.

3. What exactly is "lending at interest"?

Before laying out some principles and getting down to the arguments, it may be worth clarifying exactly what it is we are trying to study. Lending at interest arises from a particular kind of transaction, these days usually monetary, between a lender and a borrower – a "debt contract." These transactions differ from the very simplest kinds of economic transactions in one important respect. While the simplest transactions involve an exchange between a seller and a buyer at a particular point in time, with lending and borrowing there is a deliberate delay in the stages of the exchange.

For example, in a basic loan (the simplest kind of debt contract), the lender gives the borrower a sum (known as the principal) at the beginning of the contract. Then, after a certain agreed period of time, the borrower gives it back, plus a charge – the interest payment.

What the loan allows the borrower to do is *effectively* to transfer future income into the present – at a price (the interest charge). But it is important to remember that it is not possible to *actually* transfer income over time! The *actual* transfers take place at the beginning and end of the loan period and are simply movements of funds between people in whatever economic circumstances then pertain. There is a transfer from lender to borrower at the beginning of the loan period and a transfer back again at the end.

The terms of the loan contract, set at the beginning of the loan period, will depend on the expectations of how things will be at end. A key component of these terms will specify what happens if the borrower *defaults* – that is, what happens if the borrower is unable or unwilling to repay the loan. If the loan is *secured,* then the lender can use whatever it was secured against to recover some, all, or in extreme cases, more than, his principal, plus any interest owed. Someone defaulting on mortgage payments, for example, is at risk of having their home 'repossessed' by the lender. Other forms of penalty may apply for both secured and unsecured loans, depending upon the particular debt contract. These may include various forms of legal sanctions. For example, the lender may sue the borrower in an attempt to recover the debt. Before 1869 in the UK, as readers of Charles Dickens will know, those who failed to pay debts could find themselves in the notorious "debtors prisons." Imprisonment for unpaid debt still exists in one form or another in a number of countries. Historically, default has often resulted in various forms of slavery or bondage. For example, "peonage" is a form of involuntary servitude, sometimes (especially in pre-civil war United States) associated with workers being compelled by contract to pay their creditors in labour. Unscrupulous lenders may of course use a number of additional heavy-handed methods to recover debts in the event of default – or they may simply exact a punishment (even death) to deter future default.[20]

It is of course possible to legislate against heavy penalties for default without necessarily banning debt contracts completely (by explicitly legislating against slavery, for example, or by introducing some form of limited liability protection). But even if the penalty for default is limited, the possibility of default remains one of the most significant characteristics of a debt contract, and this will play an important role in our analysis below. For the moment, we shall simply note for future reference that both borrower *and lender* face some sort of risk because of the possibility of default. The borrower obviously faces the risk of penalty in the event of default. But the lender also faces the risk of failing to recover the debt.

3.1. Debt compared to rental

It may be helpful for future reference to compare debt contracts with rental contracts. There are some similarities. Rental contracts also involve transfers over time. At the beginning of a rental agreement or contract, the owner of some resource (a house, a car, land, machinery, etc.) transfers the *usage rights* to a lessee. These usage rights then

---

[20]   Shylock insisting upon his "pound of flesh" in *The Merchant of Venice* being one
       notorious and controversial example.

return to the lessor at the end of the agreement. The charge for the usage rights is the rental payment. Comparing this to a debt contract, we could perhaps describe the interest paid under a debt contract as the price paid for the 'usage rights' for the sum that has been loaned. However, the kind of risk faced in a rental contract may be different to that in a debt contract.[21] For example, in the event of default, it is usually straightforward for the lessor to recover whatever was rented – it cannot be used up in the same way that an unsecured monetary loan can be.

3.2. Debt compared to equity

An interest bearing loan is of course not the only way for an individual or organisation to raise money. Through 'equity financing,' for instance, a company issues shares of its stock and receives finance in return to invest in the business. Effectively, they are selling off a share of the company's future income stream. This is quite different from debt financing, especially in that there is no risk of default.

So consider the following three ways in which an entrepreneur might be enabled to finance a new project:

1. An interest bearing loan (debt financing).

2. A sale of shares of stock (equity financing).

3. A gift or grant.

Broadly speaking, the risk faced by the entrepreneur decreases the further down the list one gets. The most advantageous arrangement would obviously be the third one, if it were available. The second

---

[21] But not necessarily. If we compare a rent-to-buy arrangement for a house, for example, to a situation where that same house is purchased under a loan secured upon it (a mortgage), then the differences would be largely technical. Likewise, a standard rental agreement is in effect very similar to a so-called 'interest only' mortgage. The main difference would be who holds legal ownership of the property during the term of the arrangement — this having consequences in terms of responsibilities for upkeep, maintenance etc.

involves a loss of a *proportion* of future income (which could end up higher or lower than the fixed amount needed to service a loan), but there is no risk of penalty from default. On the other hand, there may be disadvantages from the second option, in terms of loss of control over the business.

The risk faced by the financer, broadly speaking, increases the further down the list one gets – rising to a risk of loss of 100% for a grant or gift, of course! One consequence of this is that there may be situations, especially for new businesses with no proven track record, where a grant would not be forthcoming and sale of shares of stock would not raise the required funds, but where a loan might be available. Because the administration of equity finance is more complex, it may also be less cost-effective for funding small businesses.

What is most favourable to the entrepreneur in terms of risk and return is therefore not aligned with what is favourable to the financer. The arrangement they come to will depend upon the particular market or bargaining conditions pertaining at the time. How much we can say about the "fairness" or "justice" of such an arrangement is an issue we shall return to later, in Section 5.1.1.

3.3. Debt in the ancient world

The legislation of the Mosaic Law and the commentary of the Prophets was made in an economic world in some ways quite different from ours, but in some ways similar. The differences are even more stark outside the ancient Greco-Roman world in the economies of the ancient Near East. Moses Finley describes such economies like this:

> The Near Eastern economies were dominated by large palace- or temple-complexes, who owned the greater part of the arable land, virtually monopolized anything that can be called "industrial production" as well as foreign trade (which includes inter-city trade, not merely trade with foreign parts), and organized the economic, military, political and religious

life of the society through a single complicated, bureaucratic, record-keeping operation for which the word "rationing," taken very broadly, is as good a one-word description as I can think of.[22]

However, "I do not wish to over-simplify," he continues; "there were private holdings of land in the Near East, privately worked; there were 'independent' craftsmen and pedlars in the town."[23] Albert Olmstead goes much further, commenting that the tablets of 7-5th century Babylonia reveal "a remarkably modern system of doing business. [...] Landed properties, houses, animals, even slaves were bought on credit."[24] There is evidence too, despite the prohibition of Deuteronomy 23:19, of intra-Jewish interest-bearing loan contracts in both Aramaic (from a 5th century Jewish colony on the island Elephantine) and Greek (the Tebunis Papyri 817 [182BC] and 818 [174BC]).[25]

In the Babylonian period (1900-732BC), Mesopotamian interest rates were capped by the Code of Hammurabi at 33⅓% for loans of grain and 20% on loans of silver. The normal rate on silver loans seems to have been between 10 and 20%. In the neo-Babylonian Empire (625-539BC), the maximum rate on barley loans was reduced to 20%. After the Persian conquest of 539BC there is some evidence that 40% became a common rate of interest in Babylonia.[26] These suggest higher rates than would usually be experienced in modern economies, perhaps because money markets remained relatively undeveloped until the middle ages. Whatever the

[22] M.I. Finley, *The Ancient Economy* (Sather Classical Lectures 48; Berkeley: University of California Press, 1985, c1973), p 28.
[23] Finley, *The Ancient Economy*, p 28-29.
[24] A.T. Olmstead, *History of the Persian Empire: Achaemenid Period* (Chicago: University of Chicago Press, 1948), pp 82-85 Quoted in Morris Silver, *Prophets and Markets: The Political Economy of Ancient Israel* (Social Dimensions of Economics; Boston: Kluwer-Nijhoff, 1983), p 66.
[25] Silver, *Prophets and Markets*, p 68.
[26] These estimates come from Sidney Homer, *A History of Interest Rates* (New Brunswick: Rutgers University Press, 1963), pp 30-31.

reason, these would have been very high rates for *individual* debtors in financial difficulty to bear, which may partly explain the repeated biblical polemic against such practice (Section 5.1 below).

3.4. *Debt in modern economies*

The practice of lending and borrowing has become immensely complex in developed economies. Nevertheless, we can identify two *main* reasons (among many other possibilities) why people might choose to borrow money at interest. First, from a producer point of view, and as we have already begun to discuss in Section 3.2 above, someone might borrow in order to fund investment, much as they might have in the ancient world. This could be, say, research into a certain kind of technological innovation. The expectation is that the investment will yield a return, a future stream of profits, which can be used to pay off the loan. A loan is of course not the only way to fund such investment. However, the availability of loans among the other options extends the overall possibilities for investment.

Second, from a consumer point of view, borrowing can be used to change someone's pattern of consumer expenditure over time. Shifting consumption into the future by saving is relatively straightforward. But being able to borrow allows consumers to shift consumption in the other direction: from the future into the present (at a cost).[27] They may do this to deal with special circumstances (e.g. medical expenses), or simply to smooth their consumption over time. People tend to have low incomes when young, higher incomes in middle age and then no income when old. Saving and borrowing are mechanisms through which they can spread this more evenly over their life cycle.

The interest rate that pertains in a market economy depends upon a huge number of complex factors. However, we may say in general that real interest rates (that is, adjusted for inflation) will tend

---

[27] We shall return very briefly to the ethics of *borrowing* below, Section 6.1.

to respond to events which affect peoples' current consumption plans relative to what the economy can currently supply. A natural disaster, for example, reduces what the economy can currently supply. Current consumption plans have to adjust downwards and this will be reflected in a rising interest rate: saving goes up, borrowing goes down, and so does consumption. Or suppose a nation discovers oil off its coast. Consumers become hopeful about future prosperity. They want to consume more now. But in the short-run there is no more to consume. As before, current consumption plans have to adjust downwards, reflected in a rise in interest rates.[28] (This is one reason why growing economies will *tend* to have higher interest rates compared to other economies experiencing lower growth at the same point in time.)

4. Some guidelines and principles of biblical ethics

Before we turn to the biblical arguments, it will be wise to be clear about the guidelines and principles under which this study will be conducted. As suggested above (in Section 2), the first two of these are *interpretive* guidelines. The second two are principles of biblical ethics that we shall find exemplified in the biblical instruction on charging at interest.

4.1. The on-going significance of the Mosaic Law

There is some data in the New Testament on charging at interest, as we shall see. However, the bulk of the biblical material on charging at interest lies in the Old Testament and the bulk of that in the Mosiac Law. This immediately raises a potential problem because of course Christians differ in the significance they place on the Mosaic Law.

---

[28] Steven E. Landsburg, *The Armchair Economist: Economics and Everyday Life* (New York: Free Press, 1993), pp 181-87.

Those in Reformed circles will be relatively happy to take it seriously as morally binding. Certainly, when Christians are exhorted by Paul to "fulfil the Law" (Romans 8:4; 13:8-10; Galatians 5:14) in practical expressions of love, they it do in Christ, by the power of the Spirit. But Paul's ethics draw upon the moral content of the Law without embarrassment, explicitly and implicitly.[29] In other words, it would seem that the moral content of the Law, read through its fulfilment in Christ, is used by the Spirit to equip the believer for every good work (cf. 2 Timothy 3:16-17).

However, even those, such as Brian Rosner, who would say that Christians do not relate to the Mosaic Law "*as law*," having "died to it and been freed from it" would give some on-going significance to the Mosaic legislation. The Law of Moses still functions as "wisdom for living."[30] Most parties, then, seem to agree that the Mosaic commands remain relevant for Christian ethics.

4.2.   *Perspectives*

Aquinas' anatomy of moral action divides an act into three: first, the act itself, which is classified according to its "object"; second, the "circumstances" of the act, which determine its wider consequences; and third, the "end" of an act, which is the subjective motivation behind it. He argues that all three features of a human act are relevant to whether it is "good."[31] That is, actions can be good or bad, consequences can be good or bad, and people can be good or bad – and the three cannot be separated. A contemporary restatement of this can be found in John Frame's "perspectivalism." We need to

---

[29]   "[T]he distinction between ceremonial and moral [though not quite Pauline] is not without a point, since Paul does think the (moral, patently not the ceremonial) commands of the Mosaic law embody the expectations of goodness inherent in the human condition. And Christians, too, are to do the 'good.'" Stephen Westerholm, *Perspectives Old and New on Paul: The 'Lutheran' Paul and His Critics* (Grand Rapids, Michigan: Eerdmans, 2004), p 437.

[30]   Brian Rosner, "Paul and the Law," *JSNT* 32, no. 4 (2010): p 418.

[31]   *Summa Theologica*, 2.i., Question 18.

know what God's law says about an action (the "normative" perspective), we need to know the creation-situation in which the action takes place in order to know how the law applies (the "situational" perspective), and we need to know the people performing the action (the "existential" perspective) in order to truly assess its moral status.[32]

For example, a key passage in our analysis below will be Deuteronomy 23:19-20. This is the famous Deuteronomic "double standard":

> You shall not charge interest on loans to your brother, interest on money, interest on food, interest on anything that is lent for interest. You may charge a foreigner interest, but you may not charge your brother interest, that the LORD your God may bless you in all that you undertake in the land that you are entering to take possession of it.

Thinking perspectivally reminds us to read the commands according to their original context and situation. Applying them to believers today then means thinking through the change in situation. Most importantly, it means thinking through the change in salvation-historical situation, but other changes too. As a Christian, who corresponds to the "brother" in the commands? Who corresponds to the "foreigner"? Do the economic or geopolitical differences between the ancient Near East and the 21st century make any difference? These are some of the questions we shall be addressing in Sections 5.2 and 5.3 below.

4.3. *"The principle of moral proximity"*

The principle of moral proximity is introduced by John Schneider like this:

> In brief, this principle states simply that our moral

---

[32] John M. Frame, *The Doctrine of the Knowledge of God* (Grand Rapids, Michigan: Baker Books, 1987), pp 62-75.

obligations in economic life are greater or lesser in proportion to their moral proximity to us.[33]

Or, to put it more completely, if someone has high "moral proximity" to me, they are relationally close (I know them or I have some other sort of personal contact with them) and I have relatively high levels of obligation towards them in terms of love and service. If someone has low moral proximity to me, then they are relatively distant relationally – perhaps anonymous or unknown. I act in such a way as to do them good, insofar as my actions have any bearing on their lives. But I am not obligated to them to the same degree.

The principle of moral proximity is really just a humble acknowledgment of our creaturely finitude. It is *physically* impossible to love everyone in the world equally, in exactly the same way. We are not called to. We are called to love our *neighbours*. While Paul does say "Let us do good to everyone" (Galatians 6:10), he does not mean us to do so in a uniform way. Immediately he qualifies what he has just said, adding, "and especially [*malista*] to those who are of the household of faith." We are social, family, community creatures, relating to relatively small numbers of people. Our obligations of love and service are higher for those close to us, or who come close to us – those who cross our path.

For example, the answer to the question "Who is my neighbour?" implied by the parable of the Good Samaritan in Luke 10:25-37 is not, as is sometimes said, "everyone" but rather, *"anyone."* Jesus does not describe a man who loves everyone in the world equally. He describes a man who unexpectedly loves (at personal risk and cost) a needy person who comes across his path even though they might normally be thought of as enemies.

So, certainly, "neighbours" should not be separated from "enemies." This was Jesus' corrective to wrong teaching on the second great commandment. "You have heard [from your teachers]

---

[33] John R. Schneider, *The Good of Affluence: Seeking God in a Culture of Wealth* (Grand Rapids: Eerdmans, 2002), p 88.

that it was said, 'You shall love your neighbour and hate your enemy.' But I say to you, Love your enemies and pray for those who persecute you" (Matthew 5:43-44, ESV). But "neighbours, including enemies" still does not encompass everyone without exception. Indeed, to be an "enemy" *usually* implies a degree of relational proximity. My enemies generally know me and I know them. And, yes, I should love them. Indeed, the gospel of Jesus Christ opens up possibilities of love and forgiveness towards my enemies that were not there before.

The principle could of course be abused. We might use it as an excuse to stop our ears to the cries of the suffering poor in the world. However, rightly understood, it is morally liberating. An impossible burden is replaced by a genuine opportunity to serve. Within our social orbit, there is a sphere of relationships where love and service really can make a difference. What is more, the principle helps us to respond to the more distant cries of suffering more effectively. Rather than anonymously showering the impoverished with money from a distance (which never quite gets to the people it should, or helps in the way we would like, and sometimes does more harm than good), we act first to reduce the moral distance. We draw people close, inviting them into our homes – as in Luke 14:13. Or we *join* the distant community that needs help, becoming their close neighbours. Where such things are difficult or impossible, we give through channels where the relational and moral proximity is higher – through local churches in affected regions, for example.

Turning back to the issue of charging interest on loans, we shall be arguing in what follows that the biblical teaching exemplifies the principle of moral proximity. To those with high moral proximity to us (including enemies, Luke 6:34-35) we give freely or lend without interest. But to those with very low moral proximity, so long as we are sure there is no danger of exploitation, we may lend with interest and still do them good by giving them something they want.

4.4.   "The doctrine of carefulness"

In his profoundly thorough treatment of Christian ethics, *The Doctrine of the Christian Life*, John Frame introduces what he calls "the doctrine of carefulness" as one important principle whereby relatively specific prohibitions in the Bible are given wider applicability – with implications for situations which are similar but not mentioned explicitly. The specific prohibition not to murder (Exodus 20:13, Deuteronomy 5:17), for example, is taken to imply a *carefulness* to avoid the loss of life. A lack of carefulness, such as an axe head not firmly attached to its shaft, has serious consequences (Deuteronomy 19:4-7). One should build a railing around the flat roof of a new house, lest one incur bloodguilt should someone fall from it (Deuteronomy 22:8).[34]

We can extend the principle to issues not directly addressed in the Scriptures. For example, the practice of abortion may be felt by some not to be directly covered by the prohibition of murder. While most Christians would be sure from the Scriptures that an unborn child has the necessary degree of personhood, there may be some who are not 100% sure. But, likewise, the same people cannot be 100% sure that an unborn child does not! Indeed, it is much more than a *bare* possibility than any unborn child *does* have a sufficient degree of personhood. The doctrine of carefulness then tells against abortion.

Frame describes a public debate with a colleague who argued that because one cannot prove for sure from the Bible than an unborn child is a person from conception, abortion might be permissible in extreme cases. Frame asked the audience to imagine that he and his opponent (whom he calls "Prof. Gottfried") are on a hunting trip:

> Anyway, the story went that we separated at some place in the woods. Then I saw a rustling in the bushes, and I raised my gun, thinking that my deer was in the vicinity. But the thought came to me: What if the movement is not a deer, but is actually Prof. Gottfried? I cannot prove that the movement is caused by a person; certainly I cannot prove that from

---

[34] John M. Frame, *The Doctrine of the Christian Life* (A Theology of Lordship; Phillipsburg: P&R, 2008), pp 686-90.

Scripture. So, on Gottfried's principle, I would be free to shoot first and ask questions later. But of course every Christian (certainly including Prof. Gottfried) would repudiate such an act. When in doubt, we avoid any action that might destroy human life.[35]

Similarly, *when in doubt*, we avoid any action that might harm someone in lesser ways to.

We shall be arguing that this doctrine or principle of carefulness is at work in Deuteronomy 23:19-20. Lending at interest is an activity that *can* harm people. The legislation, we shall argue, limits the possibility of harm by restricting the activity to lending at interest to foreigners.

5. A biblical ethics of lending and borrowing at interest

5.1. Against lending at interest to the poor

The biblical texts are crystal clear that it is wrong to charge interest on loans made to address the short-term economic necessity of the poor, and fierce in their condemnation of those who do so. Lending at interest can cause harm. The legislation begins in Exodus 22:

> If you lend money to any of my people with you who is poor, you shall not be like a moneylender to him, and you shall not exact interest from him. If ever you take your neighbour's cloak in pledge, you shall return it to him before the sun goes down, for that is his only covering, and it is his cloak for his body; in what else shall he sleep? And if he cries to me, I will hear, for I am compassionate. (Exodus 22:25-27, ESV)

---

[35]   Frame, *The Doctrine of the Christian Life.* p 725.

There is similar legislation in Leviticus 25:

> If your brother becomes poor and cannot maintain himself
> with you, you shall support him as though he were a stranger
> and a sojourner [Hebrew: *ger*], and he shall live with you.
> Take no interest from him or profit, but fear your God, that
> your brother may live beside you. You shall not lend him your
> money at interest, nor give him your food for profit. I am the
> LORD your God, who brought you out of the land of Egypt to
> give you the land of Canaan, and to be your God. (Leviticus
> 25:35-38, ESV)

This is then echoed in Proverbs 28:8:

> Whoever multiplies his wealth by interest and profit gathers it
> for him who is generous to the poor. (ESV)

The "poor" in the Exodus text are those "without (sufficient) property
and therefore dependent on others" (HALOT, *s.v.*). In the Leviticus
text, they are people who have "become destitute." They are unable to
maintain themselves. In Proverbs, they are the "helpless." It is
therefore implied that the poor are seeking loans in these scenarios in
order to deal with their immediate need or necessity – simply to
survive.

In Ezekiel 18:5-13, the prophet commends the one who "does
not lend at interest or take any profit" (18:8, 17) and condemns the
one who "lends at interest and takes a profit" (18:13). This could refer
to lending at interest to a "brother," as in Deuteronomy 23:19-20
(Section 5.2 below). But the context suggests the condemnation of
someone who also oppresses, robs, denies someone back the pledge
for a loan and denies the needy food and clothing (18:7, 12). In
Ezekiel 22:12, taking interest and profit is linked to making "gain of
your neighbours by extortion."

We shall describe the practice of lending at interest to the
poor in these texts as *exploitative* lending.

5.1.1.   Defining "exploitative".

It is actually quite difficult to pin down a precise definition of "exploitative" economic behaviour. For example, "predatory lending" is defined by the US General Accounting Office as "cases in which a broker or originating lender takes unfair advantage of a borrower, often through deception, fraud, or manipulation, to make a loan that contains terms that are disadvantageous to the borrower."[36] But to clarify what this might mean in practice the report then goes on to identify in painstaking detail a whole host of practices that might be associated with predatory lending, such as:

1. Excessive fees "that greatly exceed the amounts justified by the costs of the services provided and the credit and interest rate risks involved."

2. Excessive interest rates "that far exceed what would be justified by any risk-based pricing calculation."

3. Single-premium credit insurance, which "unnecessarily raises the amount of interest borrowers pay."

4. Lending without regard to ability to pay, leading to quick foreclosures, (sometimes where payments have exceeded monthly income).

5. "Loan flipping": repeated refinancing for which high fees are charged with no benefit to borrower.

6. Fraud and deception.

7. Prepayment penalties, when used to trap borrowers in high-cost loans

8. Balloon payments, where loans contain a final balloon payment the borrower is unlikely to be able to afford.

---

[36]   Clough, Higginson, and Parsons, "Usury," 5, quoting from a USGAO paper, *Consumer Protection:Federal and State Agencies Face Challenges in Combating Predatory Lending*, GAO-04-280, Washington, D.C.: General Accounting Office (2004), URL:<http://www.gao.gov/cgi-bin/getrpt?GAO-04-280>, p 18.

However, even with such a detailed list, there are difficulties. What, exactly, constitutes "excessive" fees and rates in points 1 and 2? What is "justified" relative to costs? And even if one could pin these vague terms down more precisely, would the resulting criteria really capture what it means for a transaction to be "exploitative"? For example, imagine a situation where one party in a transaction has relatively exclusive rights to something desired by the other party (e.g. they have monopoly power if a seller, monopsony power if a buyer – or something close to these in a local situation). This would give them extraordinary bargaining influence, so they could make a "take it or leave it" offer, maximizing their expected return. But even under such a deal (if made honestly), the stronger party might claim to be making the weaker party "better off," in that they accept the deal rather than refuse it. Many such deals are made which are "disadvantageous" to one party, relative to the outcome in more evenly matched situations. But are they all *exploitative*?

This difficulty of defining what constitutes a "fair" and "just" contract on the one hand and what constitutes an "exploitative" contract on the other applies to all economic transactions, but not least debt contracts. For example, Luther quickly ran into difficulty with his claims that "just" (i.e. non-exploitative) transactions require a sharing of risk. Luther claimed that an entrepreneur should be able to say to a financer, 'If you want to have an interest in my profits you must also have an interest in my losses, as the nature of every transaction requires.'[37] For Luther, this ruled out simple debt contracts as unjust. However, as we have already noted, a debt contract is not risk-free from the point of view of the lender – there is some risk of loss in the event of default. Moreover, it is not at all obvious that simply transferring more risk to the lender will automatically prevent a debt contract from being exploitative. A loan shark offering an impoverished debtor "double or quits," for example, would be fine under Luther's criterion.

---

[37] Luther, "Trade and Usury 1524": p 303.

This is where going back to the biblical texts and reading them carefully helps us considerably, showing us that the main feature of exploitative behaviour is not so much the "unfair" exercise of bargaining power (although such behaviour certainly may not be ideal), but that exploitative behaviour does not respond with *compassion* in a needy situation. This is the main contrast between the moneylender and the LORD in Exodus 22:25-27. We could sum up exploitative behaviour, biblically understood, as: *responding to need with greed.*[38]

For example, the sole possessor of bread charging the maximum possible price in a famine situation ("what the market can bear") is clearly not acting with compassion. But the same person charging a more "reasonable" or "fair" price may not be either. Making the needy merely "better off than they were" is not an adequate response. The situation demands that the needy be made as better off as they can be. The bread should therefore be provided at *personal cost*, not profit. Lending without interest (or giving freely) is the monetary corollary of this.

5.2. Against lending at interest to a "brother"

Deuteronomy 23:19-20 explicitly prohibits the charging of interest within the whole Israelite community, not just lending at interest to the poor:

> You shall not charge interest on loans to your brother, interest on money, interest on food, interest on anything that is lent for interest. You may charge a foreigner interest, but you may not charge your brother interest, that the LORD your God may bless you in all that you undertake in the land that you are entering to take possession of it. (Deuteronomy 23:19-20, ESV)

---

[38] It is clear that this understanding could legitimately apply to our treatment of other 'poor' in the present world such as the addicted (gambling), those with mental illness, and so on.

"Brother" here almost certainly means "fellow countryman," as in Deuteronomy 17:15 (where the contrast is also with "foreigner" [Hebrew: *nokri*]). David commends the one obedient to this command in Psalm 15:5. Nehemiah calls the nation's leaders to stop charging interest on loans to their brothers in Nehemiah 5:7, 10. It may well be that Jesus had this text in mind when he extended the prohibition (or perhaps clarified it) to lending at interest to enemies (Luke 6:35).

Why is this prohibition stronger than that in Exodus 22:25-27 and Leviticus 25:35-38? It seems unlikely that it is because lending at interest is intrinsically wrong, given the freedom to lend at interest to "foreigners" (as we shall consider below, Section 5.3). The reason given in the text is "that the LORD your God may bless you in all that you undertake in the land that you are entering to take possession of it." It is helpful to consider the two other places in Deuteronomy where a similar promise is made. The first is Deuteronomy 14:28-29:

> At the end of every three years you shall bring out all the tithe of your produce in the same year and lay it up within your towns. And the Levite, because he has no portion or inheritance with you, and the sojourner [Hebrew: *ger*], the fatherless, and the widow, who are within your towns, shall come and eat and be filled, *that the LORD your God may bless you* in all the work of your hands that you do. (ESV)

The second is Deuteronomy 24:19:

> When you reap your harvest in your field and forget a sheaf in the field, you shall not go back to get it. It shall be for the sojourner [Hebrew: *ger*], the fatherless, and the widow, *that the LORD your God may bless you* in all the work of your hands. (ESV)

In both these cases, blessing follows an expression of generosity to the needy which imitates the generosity of the LORD. It may well be, then, that the prohibition in Deuteronomy 23:19-20 is also concerned to guarantee generosity to the needy. That is, the same underlying concern is here that governed the Exodus and Leviticus prohibitions: the danger of exploiting the poor. Those potentially seeking loans in

Israel could well have included the economically vulnerable. A safe way to protect them from exploitation was simply to ban the practice of charging interest in Israel altogether. That is, the prohibition of Deuteronomy 23:19-20 is an example of the "doctrine of carefulness" (Section 4.4 above).

Nehemiah 5:1-13 can be seen as a case study of this. Israelites were lending at interest to their Jewish brothers. Some of this may have been relatively harmless, but some was adding to the suffering of those close to starvation (5:2). The solution was to restore the prohibition.

Morris Silver claims that the ban on interest within Israel's polity would have seriously damaged their economy: It was "a blow to the Israelite economy."[39] The Judeans would have had to learn "the hard way that a blanket prohibition of interest is irrational and suicidal."[40] "At the very least [such economic reforms] would have slowed Israel's rate of economic growth."[41] However, this is to underestimate both the productive potential of non-contractual, family-like relationships of trust between people of close moral proximity, and the power of God to bless those who act generously in such relationships. The expressed desire of the LORD in Deuteronomy is that the nation stand out as prosperous among their neighbours because of their obedience: "The LORD will open to you his good treasury, the heavens, to give the rain to your land in its season and to bless all the work of your hands. And you shall lend to many nations, but you shall not borrow" (Deuteronomy 28:12, ESV; cf. 15:6). It may be that the fledgling Christian community of Acts 4 experienced a similar blessing from mutual generosity, such that "there was not a needy person among them" (Acts 4:34, ESV).

So if it is wrong to lend at interest to "brothers," then under any hermeneutic (and certainly under the "perspectival" approach

---

[39] Silver, *Prophets and Markets*, p 237.
[40] Silver, *Prophets and Markets*, p 241.
[41] Silver, *Prophets and Markets*, p 242.

taken here), we are bound to ask at some point: who then are the "brothers" corresponding to the Christian? Alongside working out the new covenant equivalent of "foreigners" this is of course a vital question for our study. Many of the Church Fathers (including Cyprian, Ambrose and Chrysostom) thought that by "brothers" we should read "everyone." Aquinas agreed:

> The Jews were forbidden to lend upon interest to their brothers, that is to say, to their fellow Jews. What we are meant to understand by this is that lending upon interest to any man is wrong in itself, in so far as we ought to treat every man as a brother and neighbour, especially in the epoch of the Gospel.[42]

This of course requires that in the epoch of the gospel the category "foreigners" disappears completely. However, even apart from this, to say "brothers" equals "everyone" seems an unlikely equation. The term "brothers" in the New Testament typically refers to *Christian* brothers (or sisters) – disciples of Jesus, as in Matthew 12:46-50 and repeatedly in the book of Acts. Given Luke 6:35, we should add known enemies to this group, and perhaps other kinds of neighbour. However, even "neighbour" in the New Testament, as we have argued above (Section 4.3), does not include everyone equally without exception. We would do well to be faithful to the sense of "brother" in Deuteronomy 23:19-20. This is a restricted group, a group of "fellow-countrymen" related by Land and kin – a group with high "moral proximity," as we have put it. We should be cautious about universalizing such a group without better reasons than the ones Aquinas supplies.

Having said that, we should also want to be faithful to the element of carefulness in Deuteronomy 23:19-20. To protect the poor within Israel's polity, lending at interest is denied to those who are not poor. *Any application of this biblical teaching in a New Testament context should therefore also exhibit a similar concern to protect the*

---

[42]   *Summa Theologica*, 2.ii, Question 78, Article 1.

poor and encourage generous compassion. Should we then extend "brother" to "everyone" for this reason? Well, the Deuteronomic legislation implies it was not necessary to go so far at the time, so it may well not be so now. However, we should also remember that most modern economies have extensive statutory frameworks to address the issue of exploitation (financial regulation, limited liability, anti-slavery legislation and bankruptcy laws, etc.). This is far from saying that exploitative lending is not a problem today – clearly it still is, and especially as we engage with the developing world – just that the economic situation has changed, and we need to take that into account (see under Section 4.2 above). There may also be reasons to be careful *not* to limit lending at interest too far – also for the sake of the poor. We shall return to this possibility in Section 6.2 below.

5.3. *The freedom to lend to a "foreigner"*

In Deuteronomy 23:19-20, charging interest is permitted in certain circumstances. Although you may not charge your brother interest, *you may charge a foreigner interest.* There is a similar brother-foreigner distinction in Deuteronomy 15:3:

> You may require payment from a foreigner, but you must cancel any debt your brother owes you. (NIV)

The 'foreigner' in both texts is a *nokri.* In Deuteronomy, such a person should be distinguished from the "sojourner" [Hebrew: *ger*], as in Deuteronomy 14:21:

> You shall not eat anything that has died naturally. You may give it to the sojourner [*ger*] who is within your towns, that he may eat it, or you may sell it to a foreigner [*nokri*]. (ESV)

A *ger* is a foreigner who *may* have become a proselyte, but there is no evidence in these texts that this was necessarily so.[43] Rather, the distinction is that the *ger* is the foreigner who lives "within your

---

[43] As Paul Mills concedes, *Interest in interest.* p 5.

towns"; in contrast to the *nokri* who does not. The *ger,* as we have already seen in some of the texts above (Leviticus 25:35; Deuteronomy 14:28-29, 24:19), therefore has a close moral proximity to the Israelites. The *ger* is treated like the fatherless and the widow if they fall on hard times – like a "brother," in fact. It is apparent from Deuteronomy 23:19-20 that the *nokri* does not fall into this category.

So why is lending to a "foreigner who does not live with you" in Deuteronomy 23:19-23 permissible?

Is it because lending at interest is intrinsically wrong, but this a concession to hard-heartedness, as with aspects of the divorce laws? This seems very unlikely, because there is no such concession for the *ger,* the foreigner who lived among them. The concessions on divorce were also designed to *limit* the ill effects of sin. But if this were a "concession" it would rather *encourage* the practice, albeit at a distance.

Is lending to a "foreigner who does not live with you" acceptable because lending at interest is intrinsically wrong, but such a foreigner is an enemy, and it is therefore OK to harm him? Again, this is very unlikely. There is no suggestion in Deuteronomy that the *nokri* is to be treated as an enemy. Indeed, as we have seen, if he comes close and takes up residence, he is to be treated as a brother.

Could there be some other reason for the concession compatible with lending at interest being intrinsically wrong? Paul Mills argues that the distinction between brother and foreigner in Deuteronomy 23:19-20 was there to "draw attention to the righteous nature of Israel's law and so act as a sign to the nations of the wisdom of Israel's God."[44] Furthermore, "it seems reasonable to suppose that one of the reasons for the Deuteronomic exception was to help to create a feeling of social solidarity between all those living within the borders of Israel."[45] This suggests that the Israelites were to do something harmful to the foreigner, and therefore *wrong,* in order to

---

[44]   Paul Mills, *Interest in interest.* p 25.
[45]   Paul Mills, *Interest in interest.* pp 28-29.

highlight something that was *right* within their own polity. This would make it a very extraordinary ethic, without parallel in the Law. If something is wrong, then the Law is consistent in saying that it should not be done – even if it were to place Israel at an apparent disadvantage with respect to the nations around them.[46]

It would seem, then, that the Deuteronomic exception implies lending at interest is *not* intrinsically wrong, and there does exist a category of "lending at interest to a foreigner" where the transaction may be of mutual benefit. And we can understand this. If Hiram, a rich *nokri* from Tyre comes to me requesting a loan, happy to compensate me, so that he can, say, fund the purchase of a merchant ship, from which he expects to make many future profits, why should I deny him?

It is at this point that we need to take into account the unique geopolitical situation of Israel when the permission was given. What kind of person would the *nokri* be? Is he likely to have been needy, recently impoverished or helpless, as in the "poor" we considered in Section 5.1? No, a person in such a condition is very unlikely to travel to Israel to ask for help. Unlike someone from within Israel's borders, there is negligible chance that he is economically vulnerable – which is why we do not see the "doctrine of carefulness" applied to foreigners here as we did with the "brothers" in Section 5.2. The same argument explains why the *nokri* is not included within the addition protection of the debt-cancellation provisions of Deuteronomy 15:3. Is he a *neighbour* (either a "brother" or an "enemy"), in close moral proximity to the potential lender, as in Section 5.2? No, by definition he is not – he is a *nokri*, a foreigner who does not live among them. It is therefore reasonable to conclude that the "foreigner" encompasses everyone who is not included in the categories "poor" or "neighbour (brother or enemy), in close moral proximity." Although the

---

[46] Contra Paul Mills, *Interest in interest* p 29. Note also that not charging interest and extending debt cancellation to foreigners would not make Israel quite as vulnerable to exploitation as Mills suggests. They could simply not offer loans in the first place.

geopolitical profile of this group changes as the people of God become a global entity under the gospel of Jesus Christ, it remains a valid (and non-empty) category.

It therefore remains permissible to lend at interest to the person who is not poor and who is not in close moral proximity to the lender. There is no biblical teaching that totally bans all usury, as Calvin said. Lending at interest is godly practice in some circumstances.

6. Detailed application

6.1. Private practice

Consider first a little thought experiment. Suppose a Christian finds herself inheriting a car. Now, there are various options available to her. She could keep the car ("consume" it herself). She could give the car away. She could lend the car without charge to successive people (missionaries on furlough perhaps). She could be entrepreneurial, setting up a mini-cab business with a fellow Christian, perhaps. She could sell the car. We could, perhaps, rank these options in terms of the overt generosity associated with them. But it would be hard to say that any of them were inherently wrong. And we can imagine scenarios where any one of them might be the right and wise thing to do.

It is similar when we consider the options of what we might do with our money. There are different options, any one of which might be the right and wise thing to do in a given situation. I have been arguing in this study that one of the options open to a Christian is lending money at interest to people who are not poor and not relationally close.

Unlike a car, money also has the advantage of being divisible – we can do more than one thing with it. Picture what someone might do with any money over and above their consumption as concentric circles of action, with giving freely at the centre, like this:

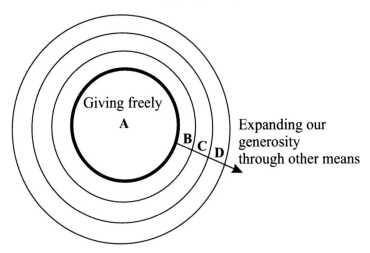

At the centre, at A, there is giving freely. But we can then expand the number of people we help by not just giving freely, also lending money without interest, as at B. When the money is returned, we can lend it to someone else and help them too. We might also want to invest some of our money for the future, helping ourselves and others be more generous in the future, as at C. These three activities should preferably be done with people in close moral proximity. But there is more we can do with our money, out at D – for the good of people not in such close proximity. We can keep our money in a bank, even in a savings account, such that it is lent out to others. We could even be more pro-active than that: perhaps lending our money in a microcredit scheme (at suitably low interest and favourable terms for the borrower).

One of the points of this picture is to emphasise that we need not think about lending at interest as an *alternative* to giving freely, lending without interest or other kinds of investment. Giving freely and generously should always be at the heart of what we do with our money. But lending at interest can be part of the package of instruments we can use to make our money work harder for the good of others – so long as we exhibit sufficient carefulness, protecting potential borrowers from harm. It allows us to extend our capacity from being a generous giver to being generous lenders too.

So it would be a mistake to misunderstand the biblical teaching on interest and cancel my deposit account at the bank. I would then be pushing interest rates up, making life difficult for any stranger wanting to borrow for legitimate reasons. Hardly an act of love! Of course, if my bank were engaging in unscrupulous exploitative lending, then I should switch banks (which would apply to my current account too). We do have a duty of carefulness to the poor. Under the Mosaic Law, this carefulness was built into the legislation. In our more open geopolitical situation, it is now incumbent upon *us* to make sure that none of our money is lent exploitatively to the poor or vulnerable.

What about borrowing? We have not said much about borrowing, partly because there is very little in the Scriptures that addresses the issue directly. We might perhaps say that once the motives of envy, greed, impatience or imprudence are removed – and we recognize that borrowing to cover mismanagement cannot really be defensible either – many of the reasons for borrowing disappear for the Christian. But, again, it is very hard to say that it is *always* wrong. If it is right to lend at interest in some circumstances, then one would have thought that it is right to borrow at interest in some circumstances.[47] Would it be wrong for a Christian to borrow to fund an entrepreneurial venture, if that were the only sensible option? Would it be wrong to borrow to pay medical expenses for an elderly relative, for example? Moreover, it is hard to see much wrong with a Christian taking out a mortgage on a house (so long as it is not excessive – driven by greed or mismanagement). Especially given that they are tied and secured loans, mortgages would seem to be a

---

[47] Although of course it would always be wrong not to honour such an arrangement, failing to repay the debt, just as it would be wrong not to honour other economic obligations: Romans 13:7-8.

relatively sensible way to fund accommodation compared to the other options.

6.2. Public policy

From what has been said, it should be obvious that Christians should want to campaign against all exploitative or dishonest economic practices, *including* those involving loans. When it comes to lending at interest, Christians should have a particular concern to protect the economically vulnerable. They will want public policy and legislation to reflect *carefulness* towards the poor.

But I also want to finish by making the case that Christians be careful to *promote* the availability of loans – also for the sake of the poor. John Schriener refers to a comment by Michael Novak: "What the poor need, Novak points out, is a legal and political environment in which they have *access to credit*, and to better education, so they can create capital" (emphasis added).[48]

Such a comment may set a few alarm bells ringing, given how much we have said above about the dangers of lending to the poor. However, we have also noted that the biblical prohibitions are focussed on loans sought by the poor *for survival*. Loans for the purpose of innovation or investment, so long as the borrower were sufficiently protected in the event of default, *could* be a different matter altogether. Promoting microcredit initiatives might be part of this, although perhaps it is still too early to judge how effective they really are relative to other types of finance.[49] Even if not, lending at interest is likely to play some sort of important role in developing economies. Historically, lending at interest has played a key role in

---

[48] Schneider, *The Good of Affluence: Seeking God in a Culture of Wealth*, p 218, referring to "The Ethical Challenges of Global Capitalism" (transcript of a debate between Ron Sider and Michael Novak), *Discernment* 8, no.1 (2001), pp 2-5.

[49] The current evidence is mixed. See, for example, Beatriz Armendáriz de Aghion and Jonathan Morduch, *The Economics of Microfinance* (Cambridge, Mass.: MIT, 2005).

promoting economic growth. And if we are serious about wanting to fight poverty, and not just paying lip-service to fighting it from the comfort of our Western prosperity, then (honest) trade and economic growth is generally a good thing. It is of course not *uniformly* good, and in practice there are many costs and injustices, as we have already noted. Moreover, I have argued elsewhere that there are limits to what economic growth can achieve – it certainly cannot achieve lasting happiness or satisfaction.[50] However, the growth arising from trade and innovation can have a powerful effect on levels of poverty. It is such growth that lifted Western economies from pre-industrial semi-rural poverty to the relative (albeit imperfect) prosperity they experience today. The mainstream view of economic historians is that banking and the availability of loans did contribute to this growth by extending the kinds of investment that could be made.[51] For a modern instance of the positive effects of economic growth on poverty, one only has to look to China. Martin Ravallion and Shaohua Chen find that between 1981 and 2001, the proportion of the population living in poverty fell from 53% to 8%.[52] China's progress against poverty may have been uneven, but that amounts to around *430 million* fewer people living in poverty – a simply staggering figure. John Lanchester describes this as "arguably the greatest economic achievement anywhere on earth, ever."[53] Western Christians could have been as generous as they liked with their free giving to the poor in China and never approached anything like such a result. As in the European industrial revolution, banking does seem to have played a role in the growth that made this possible. Financial markets remain relatively

[50] Ben Cooper, "Chasing After the Wind: The Pursuit of Happiness Through Economic Progress," *Kategoria* 13 (1999).

[51] The classic study is Rondo Cameron Crisp, *Banking in the Early Stages of Industrialization; a Study in Comparative Economic History* (New York: Oxford University Press, 1967).

[52] Martin Ravallion and Shaohua Chen, "China's (Uneven) Progress Against Poverty," *Journal of Development Economics* 82 (2007) p 2.

[53] John Lanchester, *Whoops!* p xiii.

underdeveloped in China, and finance for investment has largely come through traditional banking.[54]

If there were an all-time biblical prohibition against all kinds of interest-bearing loans, then of course we could not argue for them along these lines. But *since there is not*, then it would seem to be quite reckless to impose such a ban anyway and thereby jeopardise something with proven potential to alleviate poverty.

7. Conclusions

Is it right to lend at interest? The cynic might suggest I have given the stereotypical economist's answer: 'It depends.' (President Truman once begged, "Give me a one-handed economist! All my economists say, On the one hand on the other.") However, let me counter by saying that this should also be a typical answer for a biblical ethicist, the answer of someone sincerely trying to apply the biblical data carefully in a complex world.

We have seen clear biblical prohibitions against lending at interest to the economically vulnerable, gaining from their misfortune and failing to show compassion. I have also argued that lending at interest to those in close "moral proximity" to the lender is inappropriate. To reduce the possibility of relationally destructive exploitative lending, the Scriptures imply that lending and borrowing at interest should be restricted to relatively distant, anonymous, "non-neighbour" transactions, where both parties can be confident the trade will be beneficial and prudent for the other. But outside these restrictions there is no biblical warrant for a blanket ban on lending at interest. Moreover, this is an issue where the doctrine of carefulness cuts two ways. We should want to be careful to ensure as best we can that the poor are not exploited by interest-bearing loans. But we

---

[54] Franklin Allen, Jun Qian, and Meijun Qian, "Law, Finance and Economic Growth in China," *Journal of Financial Economics* 77, no. 1 (2005): pp 57-116.

should also want to be careful to ensure that the real world economic conditions exist whereby, so far as possible, the poor cease to be poor.

8. Bibliography

Allen, Franklin, Jun Qian, and Meijun Qian. "Law, Finance and Economic Growth in China." *Journal of Financial Economics* 77, no. 1 (2005):pp 57-116.

Calvin, J. *Commentaries on the Four Last Books of Moses Arranged in the Form of a Harmony*, Volume III. Trans. C. W. Bingham. Edinburgh: Calvin Translation Society, pp 1852-55.

——. "Letter to Claude Sachin." Pages 139–43 in *Calvin's Ecclesiastical Advice*. Eds. M. Beaty and B. W. Farley. 1545. Repr.. Edinburgh: T&T Clark, 1991.

Clough, David, Richard Higginson, and Michael Parsons. "Usury, Investment and the Sub-Prime Sector." *Association of Christian Economists Discussion Papers* DP001 (2009).

Cooper, Ben. "Chasing After the Wind: The Pursuit of Happiness Through Economic Progress." *Kategoria* 13 (1999).

Crisp, Rondo Cameron. *Banking in the Early Stages of Industrialization; a Study in Comparative Economic History*. New York: Oxford University Press, 1967.

de Aghion, Beatriz Armendáriz, and Jonathan Morduch. *The Economics of Microfinance*. Cambridge, Mass.: MIT, 2005.

Finley, M.I. *The Ancient Economy*. Sather Classical Lectures, 48. Berkeley: University of California Press, 1985, c1973.

Frame, John M. *The Doctrine of the Christian Life*. A Theology of Lordship. Phillipsburg: P & R, 2008.

——. *The Doctrine of the Knowledge of God*. Grand Rapids, Michigan: Baker Books, 1987.

Greenberg, David F. *The Construction of Homosexuality*. Chicago: University of Chicago Press, 1990.

Homer, Sidney. *A History of Interest Rates*. New Brunswick: Rutgers University Press, 1963.

Lanchester, John. *Whoops! Why Everyone Owes Everyone and no One Can Pay*. London: Penguin, 2010.

Landsburg, Steven E. *The Armchair Economist: Economics and Everyday Life*. New York: Free Press, 1993.

Luther, Martin, "Trade and Usury 1524," *Luther's Works*, Michigan: Cordordia, 2011, vol 45 pp 240-310.

Mills, Paul. *Interest in Interest: The Old Testament Ban on Interest and Its Implications for Today.* Cambridge: Jubilee Centre Publications, 1993.

Olmstead, A.T. *History of the Persian Empire: Achaemenid Period.* Chicago: University of Chicago Press, 1948.

Ravallion, Martin, and Shaohua Chen. "China's (Uneven) Progress Against Poverty." *Journal of Development Economics* 82 (2007): pp 1-42.

Renz, Thomas. "Theses on Usury Then and Now," 2008. URL: < https://sites.google.com/ site/thomasrenz02/usury>.

Rosner, Brian. "Paul and the Law." *JSNT* 32, no. 4 (2010): pp 405-19.

Schmidt, Andrew. "Matters of Interest." *The Briefing (UK Edition)* 389 (February 2011): pp 10–13.

Schneider, John R. *The Good of Affluence: Seeking God in a Culture of Wealth.* Grand Rapids: Eerdmans, 2002.

Silver, Morris. *Prophets and Markets: The Political Economy of Ancient Israel.* Social Dimensions of Economics. Boston: Kluwer-Nijhoff, 1983.

Westerholm, Stephen. *Perspectives Old and New on Paul: The 'Lutheran' Paul and His Critics.* Grand Rapids, Michigan: Eerdmans, 2004.

Lightning Source UK Ltd.
Milton Keynes UK
UKOW050440280112

186204UK00002B/192/P